WOMEN
LEADING
THE WAY

Michelle Obama

Health Advocate

by Christina Leaf

BELLWETHER MEDIA · MINNEAPOLIS, MN

Note to Librarians, Teachers, and Parents:

Blastoff! Readers are carefully developed by literacy experts and combine standards-based content with developmentally appropriate text.

Level 1 provides the most support through repetition of high-frequency words, light text, predictable sentence patterns, and strong visual support.

Level 2 offers early readers a bit more challenge through varied simple sentences, increased text load, and less repetition of high-frequency words.

Level 3 advances early-fluent readers toward fluency through increased text and concept load, less reliance on visuals, longer sentences, and more literary language.

Level 4 builds reading stamina by providing more text per page, increased use of punctuation, greater variation in sentence patterns, and increasingly challenging vocabulary.

Level 5 encourages children to move from "learning to read" to "reading to learn" by providing even more text, varied writing styles, and less familiar topics.

Whichever book is right for your reader, Blastoff! Readers are the perfect books to build confidence and encourage a love of reading that will last a lifetime!

This edition first published in 2019 by Bellwether Media, Inc.

No part of this publication may be reproduced in whole or in part without written permission of the publisher. For information regarding permission, write to Bellwether Media, Inc., Attention: Permissions Department, 6012 Blue Circle Drive, Minnetonka, MN 55343.

Library of Congress Cataloging-in-Publication Data

Names: Leaf, Christina, author.
Title: Michelle Obama : Health Advocate / by Christina Leaf.
Description: Minneapolis, MN : Bellwether Media, Inc., 2019. | Series: Blastoff! Readers: Women Leading the Way | Includes bibliographical references and index.
Identifiers: LCCN 2018033444 (print) | LCCN 2018034431 (ebook) | ISBN 9781681036663 (ebook) | ISBN 9781626179424 (hardcover : alk. paper) | ISBN 9781618915023 (pbk. : alk. paper)
Subjects: LCSH: Obama, Michelle, 1964–Juvenile literature. | African American women–Biography–Juvenile literature. | Women lawyers–United States–Biography–Juvenile literature. | African American women lawyers–Biography–Juvenile literature. | Presidents' spouses–United States–Biography–Juvenile literature.
Classification: LCC E909.O24 (ebook) | LCC E909.O24 L43 2019 (print) | DDC 973.932092 [B] –dc23
LC record available at https://lccn.loc.gov/2018033444

Text copyright © 2019 by Bellwether Media, Inc. BLASTOFF! READERS and associated logos are trademarks and/or registered trademarks of Bellwether Media, Inc. SCHOLASTIC, CHILDREN'S PRESS, and associated logos are trademarks and/or registered trademarks of Scholastic Inc., 557 Broadway, New York, NY 10012.

Editor: Kate Moening   Designer: Andrea Schneider

Printed in the United States of America, North Mankato, MN.

Table of **Contents**

Who Is Michelle Obama?

Michelle Obama is a **former** First Lady of the United States.

As First Lady, she **advocated** for children's health. She also fought for education for girls.

the Obama family

"A FULL LIFE MEANS GIVING BACK TO OUR COMMUNITY AND OUR COUNTRY." (2013)

Michelle was born in
Chicago, Illinois.
Young Michelle loved
to play outside.

She also studied hard.
Later, she attended
Princeton University.

Illinois

Chicago

After college, Michelle worked in law. She met her future husband, Barack, at a law office.

Michelle with Barack

Michelle Obama Profile

Birthday: January 17, 1964

Hometown: Chicago, Illinois

Industry: public service

Education:
- African American studies and sociology degrees (Princeton University)
- law degree (Harvard University)

Influences and Heroes:
- Fraser Robinson (father)
- Marian Shields Robinson (mother)
- Mary Tyler Moore (actress)

In later jobs, she worked to **encourage** leadership and **volunteering**.

In 2004, Barack became a **senator**. Michelle balanced her busy job and raising her daughters.

Later, Michelle worked on Barack's presidential **campaign**. Her speeches **inspired** voters.

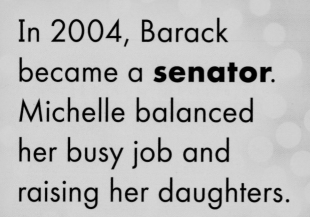

Michelle with her daughters, Malia and Sasha

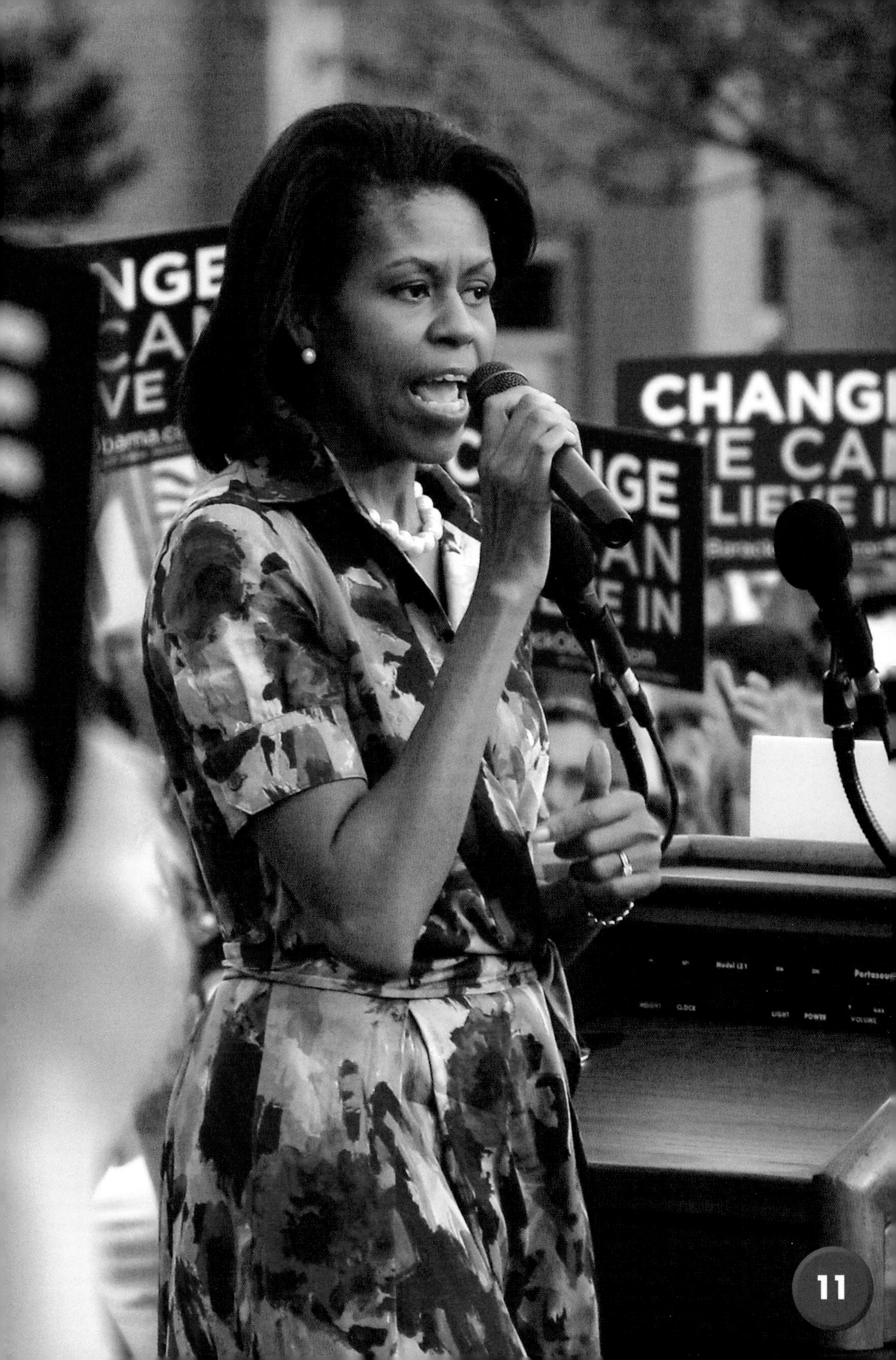
NGE
CA
VE
CHANG
E CA
LIEVE I
NGE
AN
E IN

Changing the World

In 2009, Barack became president!
The Obamas were the first
African-American First Family.

Michelle took her role as First Lady seriously. She supported **veterans**. She talked about the importance of education.

Michelle began the Let's Move! program in 2010. She wanted to help kids get healthy.

The program encouraged exercise. It made school lunches **nutritious**.

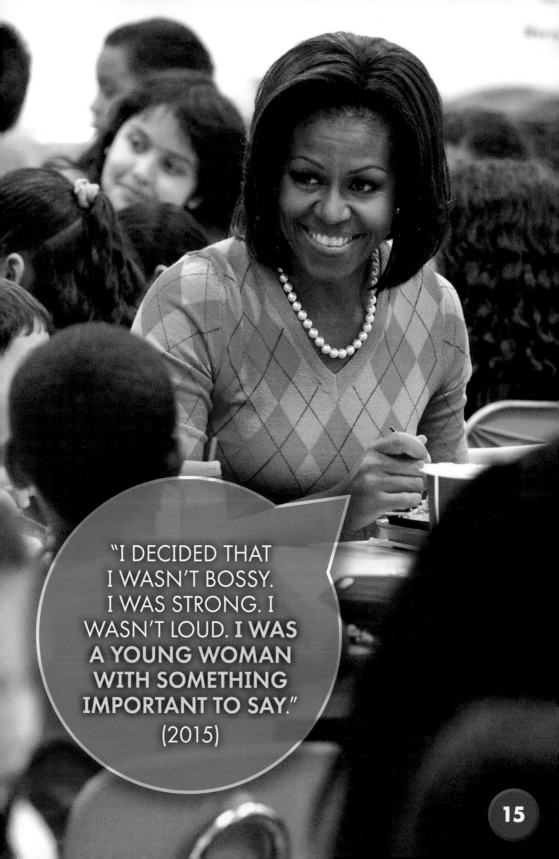

"I DECIDED THAT I WASN'T BOSSY. I WAS STRONG. I WASN'T LOUD. I WAS A YOUNG WOMAN WITH SOMETHING IMPORTANT TO SAY." (2015)

Let's Move! had challenges.
Michelle worked with businesses
to make healthier **products**.
People questioned this.

Congress also fought the program. But it brought positive changes!

Michelle's Future

Michelle is no longer the First Lady.
But she still has work to do.

Michelle Obama Timeline

1964   Michelle is born in Chicago, Illinois

1996   Michelle begins working at the University of Chicago

2009   Michelle becomes the first African-American First Lady of the United States

2010   Michelle begins the Let's Move! program

2016   Michelle's powerful speech at the Democratic National Convention makes headlines

She wants to keep changing the world.

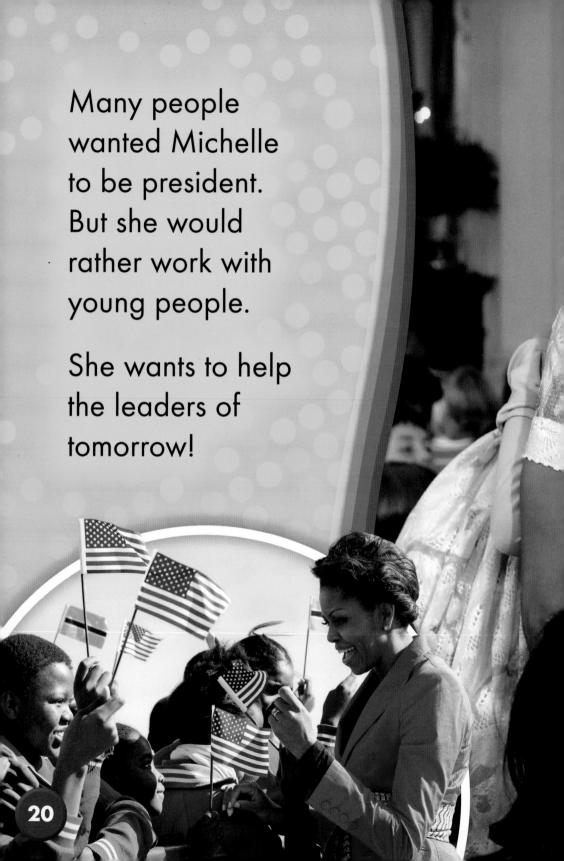

Many people wanted Michelle to be president. But she would rather work with young people.

She wants to help the leaders of tomorrow!

"I FIND HOPE
IN ALL THESE
BEAUTIFUL
YOUNG PEOPLE."
(2018)

Glossary

advocated—supported and argued for a cause

campaign—a connected series of activities that work to bring about a particular event

Congress—the group of people that makes laws for the United States

encourage—to give the help needed to accomplish a goal

former—from a time before

inspired—gave someone an idea about what to do or create

nutritious—healthy

products—things that are made or grown to be sold or used

senator—a member of the Senate; the Senate is part of Congress.

veterans—people who served in the military

volunteering—doing a service without expecting anything in return

To Learn More

AT THE LIBRARY

Corey, Shana. *Michelle Obama: First Lady, Going Higher*. New York, N.Y.: Random House, 2018.

Hansen, Grace. *Michelle Obama: Former First Lady & Role Model*. Minneapolis, Minn.: Abdo Kids, 2018.

Taylor-Butler, Christine. *Michelle Obama*. New York, N.Y.: Children's Press, 2015.

ON THE WEB

FACTSURFER

Factsurfer.com gives you a safe, fun way to find more information.

1. Go to www.factsurfer.com.

2. Enter "Michelle Obama" into the search box.

3. Click the "Surf" button and select your book cover to see a list of related web sites.

Index

The images in this book are reproduced through the courtesy of: Chuck Kennedy, front cover (Michelle); Andrei Kholmov, front cover (cafeteria); Maksim Shmeljov, front cover (vegetables); Tim UR, p. 3; Pete Souza, p. 4 (inset); Jonathan Bachman, pp. 4-5; Jim Watson, pp. 6-7; Pablo Martinez Monsivais, p. 8; EPG_EuroPhotoGraphics, p. 9; Chip Somodevilla, pp. 10 (inset), 16-17 (bottom right), 20-21; jdwfoto, pp. 10-11; Handout, pp. 12-13 (top left); 501 collection, pp. 12-13 (bottom right); Greg Fiume, p. 14 (inset); Saul Loeb, pp. 14-15; Jewel Samad, pp. 16-17 (top left); Jeff J Mitchell, pp. 18-19; AFP, p. 20 (inset); Maksim Shmeljov, pp. 22-23.